FIVE MYTHS
OF MALE
SEXUALITY

RICK GHENT

MOODY PRESS
CHICAGO

Which is right? "If it feels good, do it!" or "If it feels good, it must be wrong"?

Is it "Experience makes a man a better lover" or "Save yourself for marriage"?

Is it "Be strong and in control" or "Be sensitive and relational"?

Most men never get a clear, balanced view of sex and intimacy. Instead, they get a multitude of conflicting messages, each representing a partial truth.

When it comes to male sexuality, it's the age-old story of the world shouting in one ear and the church shouting in the other. At times the racket is so great that we can't even hear God. Because of this, sexual problems of various kinds are common today.

Jim's problems at work and in his marriage drove him into my counseling office. Jim had been unable to concentrate at work and was feeling very distant from his wife. He soon admitted to me what he already knew: he was thinking too much about the women at work, and many of these

3

thoughts were sexual. Jim recognized many of these thinking patterns were lustful; that is, he was obsessed with sexual thoughts and plans.

"I'm afraid that I'm losing my feelings of attraction and physical desire for my wife," Jim said. "My mind often drifts to the younger women at work, sometimes even when I'm home. These women seem to respect me and want to know me. And they even seemed to be sexually attracted to me. I'm flattered and I'm confused."

As a Christian, Jim knew his thoughts were dangerously lustful, that he was flirting with the danger of an extramarital affair. He wanted to live for Christ, but he felt torn because of his struggles.

As we talked, I learned Jim had become a Christian during college. His struggles with lust did not disappear, however. Jim found himself needing a girlfriend, and his mind seemed flooded with sexual thoughts.

"The closer I became to a woman, the more sexual the relationship became. This happened again and again with different women, and usually I would terminate the relationship out of guilt. I had heard that 'real men' were not virgins, and I really battled that concept. Often I'd excuse my behavior, thinking, *What's the big deal? I'm just a normal guy.*"

Jim married soon after college,

partly to take care of his problem with sexual temptation. Jim thought marriage would be an incredible sexual experience, a never-ending, passionate love affair.

Fifteen years later, two children and a busy career had dulled his passion. Actually, unending passion in marriage is a myth many single men bring into marriage (and many single women too). But Jim had felt uncomfortable during the past four years as he discovered his sexual desire was diminishing; now it had almost dried up. He spent less time at home and more time at work; he was growing distant from his wife. Jim wanted to enjoy the sexual relationship with his wife, but so many things got in the way and the relationship seemed to take too much work.

Because of his lack of appetite for sex in his marriage, Jim began to doubt his masculinity. He felt like less of a man than his male coworkers who boasted about their sexual exploits. Soon Jim began to pay attention to the women at work. They were young, single, and accessible, and Jim thought somehow that sex with them would be passionate, powerful, almost life-changing.

Jim wanted to rid himself of these lusts, but they tended to make the pain of his situation disappear, so he was tempted. His coworkers would tease him about being so uptight, saying that a little fling would help him out. Jim began to believe that a great sexual partner would bring him the fulfillment he deserved. His thoughts were spurred on by the movies, where Jim heard several messages about men and their sexuality: "real men" always have great sex; sex comes naturally to men; and men do not have sexual problems.

As Jim and I discussed these issues, he began to realize he had believed what our culture teaches about being male and sexual. His coworkers, the movies, and TV had Jim believing the five myths of male sexuality.

Two Faulty Views of Sex

Before we look at those five myths, we need to recognize two faulty views men hear about their sexuality. One view comes from our culture; the other, from the church.

CULTURE AND THE MEDIA

Culture teaches us that real men do not have sexual problems. For real men, pleasing women and control come naturally.

The various media portray the message consistently. Movies, television, and advertising show confident, assertive, and sexually attractive men. Men control and please women without frustration and with little rejection.

It's a faulty view, of course, and traces back in part to America's so-called sexual revolution of the sixties and seventies. The revolution supposedly freed us.

In truth, we have become enslaved to the sexual hunt, both as single men and married, hoping to find satisfaction in conquest and control. The revolution has given us media images of raw, passionate sex at every turn. The images in books, magazines, movies, and TV argue for the irresistible power of seduction and the joys of uncommitted sex. We are no longer ignorant and prudish. Our culture believes in the myth that anything goes.

Indeed, one of 1987's most popular movies showed a spurned woman so craving her lover that she pursued him to the death, in a *Fatal Attraction* both flattering and dangerous for the unfaithful husband.

The media portray men as "comfortable with everything—vaginal, oral and anal sex; sex with or without drugs; sex in public places; sex with several partners at the same time; and sex without protection against pregnancy and disease."[1] Supposedly art reflects life. Producers and executives claim the movies are portraying men as they are, comfortable with all forms of sexual activity. If movies and paperback novels often have male detectives bedding female coworkers, it's because virile men attract women, and sex is a sign of virility.

Yet other traits of men, such as faithfulness, courage, and honesty, are ignored. Movies rarely show the man who refuses the seduction because he loves his wife and children or has chosen to save himself for marriage. The message remains biased and inaccurate: the man who resists extramarital or premarital sex is uptight and unreal.

Indeed, television and movie characters—held up as heroes by our young—shed virginity like a shabby childish garment and replace it with glimmering, sweaty sensuality. Everything we see shouts clearly that virginity is abnormal and unglamorous. The adolescent who tries to abstain gets the message that he or she is hopelessly out of step.[2]

Meanwhile, men are called upon to be sensitive and nurturing , as movies portray sex as a powerful, almost violent, act.

Silver-screen sex is not a formula for true intimacy. The macho image in which a man is supposed to perform well, enjoy it immensely, and please his partner every time remains both an untruth and a roadblock to intimacy between a man and a woman.

True intimacy can occur only when we display honesty and openness about our problems and ignorance.

THE CHURCH

Shouting just as loudly about a man's sexuality is the church. Though the message may vary from denomination to denomination and from one church to another, many preachers, teachers, and even Christian parents distort what the Bible says about men expressing their sexuality.

Dean was raised in a fundamentalist Christian home where even the word *sex* was considered vulgar and dirty. Warnings against lust and sins of the flesh were familiar themes at home and at church. His parents and the pastor made normal adolescent attraction seem sinful.

Unintentionally, at age twelve Dean discovered masturbation and was energized, guilt-ridden, ashamed, and addicted all at once. With no one to talk to, Dean held the shame and confusion inside. His powerful secret isolated him from his family, friends, and God.

The masturbation became habitual, and eventually pornography became a part of the ritual. Unable to break the pattern, he went through high school and college hiding his obsession with this behavior.

Hoping to rid himself of the obsession, Dean married in his midtwenties. Although he loved his wife, he failed to find intimacy. As his hidden frustrations and problems created an emotional wedge between them, his wife withdrew sexually. Later he returned to masturbation and pornography.

As the church pounded out a single message on the filth of sex, it inadvertently had enabled Dean's problem to develop. His awakening adolescent feelings needed to be addressed. In the church's silence, the resulting vacuum was filled with improper messages from the culture.

Even the church contributes to distortion as it refuses to address the issues of sexuality or focuses on warnings rather than guidelines. The positive aspects of marital sex are commonly ignored by the church in favor of messages on the sinfulness of sex.

Many men raised in Christian homes and/or attending churches have experienced a conflict, according to Christian sex therapists Clifford and Joyce Penner, who have written *The Gift of Sex*.

The conflict was that specific instruction about sexual interactions between men and women was either absent or limited. Instruction regarding sexual involvement within marriage was lacking; at the same time, the [sermons, Sunday school lessons, and parental words] clearly warned about keeping oneself pure. Rigid rules were defined for acceptable dating habits.

The absence of positive sexual teaching, combined with the rigid rules about sexual expression lead us both to believe that sex between a man and a woman was seen by our church as very negative, even though we did not feel this.[3]

This focus on the negative issues of sex has colored men's attitudes about sex. The church could be a great place to learn about sex. A positive and balanced view of sex presented by the church would promote abstinence and healthy marital sex.

The Biblical View of Sex

Unlike certain elements of the local church, the Bible consistently presents an unrepressed, balanced view of sex. Genesis 1:27 reports "God created man in His own image, in the image of God He created him; male and female He created them."

What is the image of God? Four areas of our being are formed in the image of God: the spiritual, the intellectual, the emotional, and the relational.

First, we are *spiritual* beings. When it comes to our sexuality, we are not physical hormones waiting for release. Our sexuality is intertwined with healthy spirituality.

Second, we are *intellectual* beings, created with the ability to reason and learn. Our minds can help us learn about our sexuality. Healthy sexuality depends on clear information about physical intimacy.

Third, like God, we have feelings. God feels anger, love, compassion, joy, and sadness. We too are *emotional* beings, and our sexuality is tied to our emotions. It is destructive to separate them.

Fourth, we were created to be *relational*. We need relationships with other people. After Adam was created God declared, "It is not good for the man to be alone." So God created Eve for companionship. Adam and Eve were created in God's image. "The two shall be as one."

Our very creation shows that we are to be in relationship. Marriage, the most intimate form of relationship, is intended to help fulfill the relational need. In marriage, our sexuality allows both a meaningful and pleasurable expression of relational intimacy.

In Ephesians, Paul uses marriage as a metaphor for our relationship with Christ. He was not ashamed to illustrate the intimacy we are to share with Christ.

The Song of Songs is the most romantic and sensual book of the Bible. Solomon advocates strong sexual relationships within the confines of marriage, and with passionate words the husband declares his love in this extended Hebrew poem.

> How beautiful are your feet in sandals. . . . The curves of your hips are like jewels. . . . Your belly is like a heap of wheat fenced about with lilies. Your two breasts are like two fawns. . . . Your stature is like a palm tree. . . . "I will climb the palm tree, I will take hold of its fruit stalks." May your breasts be like clusters of the vine. (Song of Songs 7:1–3; 7–8)

Wow! That is the Word of God? While the difference in cultures may not make these exact words appropriate to whisper in your beloved's ear, this was clearly written with the attitude that sex is something beautiful which we are created to enjoy wholeheartedly.

Although the Bible clearly articulates the beauty of marital sex, we are more often exposed to the distorted truths about sex from our culture and the church. These distorted truths have grown into myths about male sexuality. The strength of a myth is often very great; we can hear it enough that, for us, it becomes truth. Let's sort through some of these myths.

Myth #1: Real Men Want
Sex Anytime, Anywhere

Hollywood recently has been producing more psychosexual thrillers. These movies perpetuate the fable about men and their voracious sexual appetites.

The movie *Fatal Attraction*, nominated for an Academy Award as best picture of 1987, begins with the stereotype of the happy family: happy little girl, beautiful and adoring wife, even a trustworthy and handsome Labrador retriever. The father, played by Michael Douglas, is a busy, successful lawyer. Douglas is lured into what he considers a one-night encounter with another woman.

The unmistakable message is that it is a natural recreational alternative for a married man to have sexual relationships outside of marriage. In this bizarre case, though, what is supposed to be just fun turns into a fatal attraction by the "other woman." She wants Douglas and pursues him with an obsession. The "one-night stand" results in a cleft in the marriage and the murder of the mistress by the husband and wife.

The moral of the movie? The insuppressible desire to have sex wherever, whenever, however, and with whoever is perfectly normal, but it can get you into a lot of trouble. Dismissed as irrelevant or unlikely is the fact that an extramarital affair can devastate the marriage and bring sorrow to each person involved.

In 1992, another movie with a blatant sexual myth about men hit the theaters. In *Basic Instinct*, a man uses sex to help his lover overcome a death she is grieving.

There are two prominent messages in this movie: (1) the sexual urge is more powerful than gray matter and feelings; and (2) sex will heal the deepest pain in a woman's life.

The first message is the same as myth #1, that testosterone compels men to want sex anywhere, anytime. The second is related to myth #5, that men know how women think and feel about sex. We will discuss myth #5 later.

Moviemakers seem perceptive as they dig below the surface of the male sexuality myths and show the consequences of buying into those myths. While producers of such shows exploit the extreme for entertainment's sake, real life is not far off. Real-life victims of fatal attractions have walked into my office. Almost all these men have bought into myth #1.

Yet we are believing a myth when we think men typically want sex anywhere and anytime. The reality is that few married people have ever been unfaithful to their partners. The National Opinion Research Center (NORC) has surveyed 1,500 people about marital fidelity and found similar results in 1991 and 1993. In 1993, 16 percent of all married respondents said they had cheated on their mates, compared with 14 percent in 1991. Among men, the figures were only slightly higher: 21.3 and 21.0 percent, respectively, for the two years.[4] This means, according to the NORC surveys, that four of five married men have never cheated on their wives.

NORC research director Tom W. Smith, finding that a consistently low percentage of men and women participate in affairs, criticizes the media for misreporting and for misrepresenting poorly done surveys. "There are probably more scientifically worthless facts on extramarital relations," Smith says, "than on any other facet of human behavior."[5]

Moreover, the majority of men prefer to make their marriages work and choose to stay committed to one woman. Researcher George Barna has found that only one in four Americans "who have been married have experienced at least one divorce." The common figure of 50 percent of all marriages ending in divorce, however, is a "whopping deception."

Barna says that figure is spread by "illogical mathematics and the unthinking acceptance of this 'fact' by scholars, journalists, politicians, and public figures."[6]

Gary Bauer, director of the Family Research Council, agrees with Barna and Smith that statistics about marital fidelity and stability are distorted; Bauer notes that psychologist Joyce Brothers and researcher Sharon Hite have "stoked reports of rampant infidelity." The Family Research Council also notes that a 1987 ABC News/Washington Post poll found 89 percent of spouses faithful.[7]

Some believe that men want sex anytime because they must alleviate physical pressure. Some men have accepted the myth, thinking that if they don't alleviate the pressure, they will explode. However, seminal fluid can be reabsorbed or released through nocturnal emission. Men do not have to have sex to relieve this tension. Men do have power over their sexual drives. One can say no to his sexual urges as surely as one can say no to drugs or an excess of food. For full expression of their sexuality, men can choose to wait until marriage, which is the right time chosen by God.

What about the sexual addict, who seemingly wants sex at every opportunity? Many of the men with whom I counsel are addicted to sex. Sexual addiction is a compulsive lifestyle of seeking sexual encounters, which can affect most areas of a man's life: family, finances, and friendships.

Interestingly, in my practice and in the practices of colleagues, men who are addicted to sex commonly report that they hate what they have become but do not see a way out. As the struggles of prominent Christian men have become public, it's become evident the problem is not exclusively secular.

The guilt and pain of addiction often result in struggles with sex in the addict's marriage. Sex to the sexual addict is not self-affirming or beautiful. Sex is his drug. So even for the sex addict the myth that men want sex anytime, anywhere, and with anyone only creates greater pain.

Through counseling and with God's help, sexual addicts can overcome the uncontrolled patterns and learn to find a pleasurable and a satisfying sex life through a healthy, intimate marriage.

LOSS OF SEXUAL DESIRE

Most men recognize the connection between a healthy sex life and a healthy marriage. They understand that sex and intimacy are interconnected emotionally and relationally. Men who are having marital problems do not usually desire the sexual relationship. At that point in the marriage, a husband has less desire and sometimes even less ability to have sex. This does not mean he is less of a man or automatically less loving. It does mean the marriage is under some type of stress.

When a marriage is full of stress, conflict, and emotional problems, men can lose the desire for sex. Remember, loss of sensual desire is not a reflection on masculinity. It is normal for men to have a great desire for intercourse at times and none at others. Men who experience a loss of sexual appetite when presented the opportunity may have self-doubts about manliness and become even less sexual as a result of worrying. It is a myth that sex is just a biological function, disconnected from intellect and passion.

Men may not be interested in sex for a variety of reasons. In addition to lower desire during times of heavy stress, men can also experience decreased sexual desire due to alcohol use or physical problems. Depression also can lower sexual hunger.

Of course, responding to the myth that real men want sex anytime and anywhere requires our recognizing that the statement is false. But there's more we can do. Here are four steps, all important, that can help you have a proper attitude toward your sexual drive.

Step 1: Understand the true nature of sex. Sex was created by God as beautiful and exciting within the bounds of marriage. Sex for sex's sake is actually painful in long-term consequences. We were created for relationship. Only within a stable, secure relationship can healthy, God-designed sexuality develop.

Step 2: Accept sexual desires and thoughts as normal and good. Our sexual desires are healthy and God given, part of our identity, and even a way of being drawn into relationships. The danger comes when we let sexual desires and thoughts become an obsession. Obsession with sexual thoughts leads to lust. Lust is the desire or intent to sin sexually. Lust occurs when a man (or woman) looks at and desires to possess the person for sexual purposes, even without any action being taken. Lust hurts.

If you find yourself becoming obsessed with sex—losing working hours, study hours, or quality time in relationships while fantasizing about sex—you need to understand the reason for the obsession. Obsessing is probably your method of dealing with other painful problems in your life. As you begin to understand those problems and work through the feelings, the need to obsess will decrease.

Step 3: Accept the fact that at certain times you will have limited sexual desire. If you lack desire, you are probably normal. There is no need to question your masculinity. The lack of desire may result from stress, marital problems, depression, or a variety of other causes. If this problem continues over a period of two or more months, you may want to seek help.

Step 4: Find a friend. Most males understand these struggles. A good male friend, who will be as honest with you about his struggles, will do wonders in the battle against this myth. Seek a friend you trust, someone you can be honest with and accountable to for your thoughts, feelings, and actions.

Myth #2: Real Men Have Affairs Because of Sexual Problems in Marriage

This myth is supported in our culture by statements like these:

"If the sex in the marriage had been good enough, he would never have had the affair."

"You'd better keep him happy if you don't want him to stray."

"I was not happy with my sex life, so I had to find someone who would make me content sexually."

Monte, who has been married seventeen years, demonstrates that extramarital affairs are usually not caused by sexual problems. The early years had been very stressful for Monte and his wife, Sue. The two had grown up in Christian homes, and now they wanted a family of their own. A short ten months after their wedding they became parents. They were delighted. The baby brought such joy that they did not notice the lack of sleep, quality time, and sex in their relationship.

Four years and three children later, Monte and Sue were exhausted. As Monte put it, he was "fried." They worked hard to make ends meet. They loved their children and spent great effort on parenting. But they neglected their time with each other. Gradually they drifted apart. They kept up the front of a healthy marriage because of their involvement in church and their desire to make an impact in others' lives. Sue recognized her obligation, so they maintained a fairly steady sex life, but only as an obligation; it failed to draw the couple together.

As their children entered adolescence, new tension arose. They worked hard to be good Christians and virtuous parents—and they continued to burn out.

Monte spent more time at work to avoid some of the stress at home. There he met a recently divorced woman named Linda, who went to his church. Monte found support in the friendship. He would ask how she was doing and offered his help. Their conversations turned into lunches. The relationship grew deeper. Monte began to talk about his marriage and struggles. Linda seemed to understand him. They could talk about life, their relationship with God, and their dreams. Monte began thinking about her at work. Although he believed he would never act on his thoughts, Monte realized how much he cared about Linda.

Monte took Linda home after work one evening. She invited him in and before he knew it, he was taking her to bed. At that moment, nothing seemed more beautiful than what he felt.

Monte told Linda and himself that would not happen again, but it did. He wondered whether after seventeen years of marriage he had met the "right" person. Had God allowed this to happen? Only after several sessions did Monte recognize the underlying reasons for his fall: he had not nurtured his marriage in years and chose not to deal with his feelings and struggles in the marriage.

Only a minority of men succumb to affairs, as noted earlier; those who do, such as Monte, fall for one of three reasons. There are three types of affairs: The sexually addicted affair, the one-night stand, and the affair of the heart. All involve sin, but the long-term consequences can vary.

The most common and, in some ways, least damaging is *the one-night stand*. Men with sexual dysfunction in their marriage might seek out a one-night stand for assurance of their masculinity. They do not have the liaison simply because they want sex. Instead, these men want assurance that they are attractive and masculine.

A one-night affair can also be a passive-aggressive expression of hostility. Whether caused by the need for acceptance, a chance to escape, or mere curiosity, the pain is never worth the pleasure. However, most married couples can work through this type of affair.

Affairs of the heart, which can last from two weeks to more than a decade, are the most destructive to marriages. Although sex is involved, the affair revolves around what is perceived as love, acceptance, and respect. Typically, the man believes love and acceptance is missing in his marriage, and it is the perception of its presence in this relationship that drives him to a sexual affair.

Such affairs can begin anywhere —the workplace, health club, neighborhood, or church—whenever an emotional bond of friendship develops. Eventually a growing feeling of closeness draws the man into an illicit sexual relationship.

Once dissolved, affairs of the heart tend to have a long half-life involving grief over the deep loss. Without the difficulties of children and financial responsibilities, these affairs maintain a flawless charm and the excitement of the forbidden.

Yet despite the excitement and promise of pleasure, these affairs that are supposedly based on love typically involve pain and frustration. Sex researchers Masters and Johnson were surprised at their findings of discontent: "What tends to be amazing is that the overall pleasure of the sexual experience is less pleasurable than their marital sexual experience."[8]

Many marriages can survive an affair of the heart with a great deal of effort, often professional help, and years of rebuilding.

Some husbands enter an affair be-

25

cause of a craving for new sexual experiences. They are sexually addicted, a condition described in our discussion of myth #1. However, *the sexually addicted affair,* like the other two types of affairs, involves sins much greater than simply the act of unfaithfulness to your wife. Some of these sins include pride, self-sufficiency, lust, and apathy (ignoring the early problems in your marriage and doing nothing about them).

Biblically, we are given the freedom to divorce a spouse who has had an affair. However, divorce does not solve the issues that led to the affair.

When Monte and Sue came in for counseling, Monte described their sex life as terrible and blamed this for the affair. Through counseling, Monte realized that the emotional bank account in his marriage was overdrawn. The reason for the affair was a bankrupt marriage which Monte had stopped investing in when he started investing in the affair. His was an affair of the heart in which he thought Sue was not giving him love and acceptance. Both could participate in mending the marriage. Sue was willing to work hard along with Monte to rebuild their relationship. Their relationship grew and, years later, their sexual relationship became fulfilling.

Men have affairs to prove their masculinity, to pay back their wife, to complete the emotional affair already going and to find love and acceptance. Men seldom have affairs for sex.

DEALING WITH THE MYTH

If you are considering having an affair, are having one now, or just want to know how to fight the myth, read on.

Step 1: If the sexual part of your marriage seems shaky or has even collapsed, *realize that good sex comes through having an intimate relationship with your spouse.* Good sex is a by-product of each partner knowing and caring for the other. Direct your attention to improving your relationship, not to improving your sexual technique.

Step 2: Understand that most men have affairs to feel loved and accepted. Admitting to feelings of being misunderstood and disrespected might avoid an affair. When we can admit to God and to our wives that we don't feel understood or respected, we have taken an important step toward avoiding an affair. Talk to your wife about your feelings. As you deal with the emotional roots in your relationship, you can find the intimacy you desire within the marriage.

Step 3: Be accountable to other men. Most of us struggle with marriage and our sex lives. It is important to find friends who are both honest about their struggles and willing to call you on unhealthy ways of dealing with yours. Find a friend who will agree to pray for you about your struggle.

Step 4: Pastoral or professional counselors can be beneficial, especially for men who have affairs for sex alone. All affairs are destructive for the marriage, but the sexually-addicted affair can be most difficult to overcome. The willingness to admit your need is the first step toward a healthy sex life. Many men have had affairs and are willing to help others deal with their struggles. These men can help you understand and resolve the consequences of an affair.

Myth #3: Real Men Are Comfortable with Talking and Knowing About Sex

As a college student, I worked summers as a mountain guide for a Christian organization. I will never forget a particular all-men's backpacking trip. One night as we sat around the campfire talking about the Christian life, most of the men began to fade. Gary, a good-looking athletic guy—the kind who always gets the girls—confessed to us his problem with masturbation. Immediately the esoteric theological discussion ended. Everybody woke up. One by one, every guy around that campfire shared his own struggles with sex and masturbation.

These young healthy men had never felt comfortable talking with anyone about their sexuality. We did not come up with answers, but the openness showed us all just how uncomfortable we really are about our sexuality.

THE SEX TALK

One of the guys, Dan, recounted his dad's version of "the birds and the bees" talk. Dan was about to have his first real date in seventh grade. He was meeting the girl at the movie, and Dan's father took him there. Dan knew something was up as his father parked at the end of the parking lot. He stopped the car and put his arm across the back of Dan's seat. Dan's thoughts strayed to the beer he had stashed. *Had Dad found out about it?*

His dad began, "Dan, when I was in the Navy they told us sex was dirty. That sex was evil. Son, I want you to know sex is not evil. Have a good time tonight." That was it! That was the sex talk. Dan's dad was right: sex is good. But he gave an incomplete picture, and his inability to really discuss the issue sent a different message. Men are uncomfortable discussing sex. In fact, most men don't get any version of the sex talk from their fathers.

Very few of us feel comfortable talking about sex. Many of us have had little sex education. Oh sure, we had the *Popular Mechanics* version in junior high. We learned how everything functions, its purpose and place on our bodies. But that did very little in helping us understand our sexuality. Men tend not to be readers and find it difficult to make time to read about sex. We feel very embarrassed discussing the issue with our wives.

The fact is men are uncomfortable with knowing how sex works. We would rather have good intentions than knowledge and skill. We feel responsible to please our wives, and we believe we should somehow magically know—without studying or being taught—what does please them.

Men also believe that their masculinity is reflected by their sexual performance. Men tend to place more importance on how often they have sex, not how well it is going. And because most men believe performance demonstrates masculinity, few men would willingly admit to not knowing how to perform.

In truth, most men know little about the female anatomy. I was very naive until I needed to give advice about sexual practices. Men seldom know about foreplay—those caresses of love that arouse and prepare a woman—and after-play—the soft words and body touches that nurture a woman in her "afterglow." Sadly, few husbands know what pleases their wives; though they love their wives, they are unable to give them full physical pleasure. Most think intercourse alone is what sex is all about.

But those Hollywood actors are only performing an act. There is no magical or perfect sexual technique that will bring a woman to orgasm. Women tend to be relationally oriented in their sexuality. Orgasm is more than just a physical experience. A wife needs to feel close to her husband and loved by him. Furthermore, she needs to be free to clearly communicate her desires. This can happen in open communication with her husband. Mind reading is frustrating and inadequate as a mode of communication for fulfilling your wife's sexual desires. Ask your wife about her needs.

DEALING WITH THE MYTH

Remember, openness and education are the keys in becoming more comfortable talking and knowing about sex. Here are four practical steps.

Step 1: Admit to yourself you're uncomfortable. Tell your spouse how awkward it is for you to discuss sex. Believe that a good sex life is built on good communication. A real man will have the courage to move past his embarrassment and fear to discuss with his wife what she would enjoy in the sexual experience.

Step 2: Get educated. Stop by your local Christian bookstore and purchase a book dealing with sexual relationships in marriage. There are books on both relationships and sexual response, and both would be helpful. Choose a book to read with your spouse. Try something new.

Step 3: Realize that other men also are uncomfortable with issues about sex. Our culture pretends to be current and educated, but few of us really know what we are doing even after years of being sexually active. Real relationships do not just happen. Good sex doesn't just come naturally.

Step 4: Set up a regular meeting to discuss your sex life with your spouse. Such conversations are part of what an open, honest relationship is about—the husband and wife sharing concerns and successes. Make the sexual part of your relationship a matter of prayer as well. And if you have a close, trusted couple, perhaps talk to that couple about what has been helpful for them.

Myth #4: Real Men Dislike Communication and Emotions

We have been reared in a society that models "strong" unemotional men as "real men." Growing up, I did not see an adult male show any emotion other than anger. Clint Eastwood was the perfect example of how to be a man. Clint's one emotion was calm, cool anger. His anger always came out in revenge.

Men in our culture have gotten the message that tears are a sign of weakness. Men often feel ashamed when they have strong emotions. The myth translates that real men would have control. They never show sadness or joy. Anger, while acceptable, is always controlled and calculated.

In his appropriately titled book, *Real Men Have Feelings Too*, Gary Oliver explodes the myth that men dislike communication and emotions. The problem, he writes, is they have difficulty expressing feelings: "Men are emotional. The problem is that most men don't understand their emotions and they have not learned healthy and appropriate ways to express them (though they do express feelings in various ways)."[9]

The men I know have strong emotions and they desire to express them in ways that work. The majority of men are more than willing to learn to be open and discuss their feelings. The difficulty lies with our culture, which inhibits men from being themselves. Clint Eastwood and the American culture put great expectations on men to be the strong, silent type. Most men want to communicate and express feeling. But they aren't sure it's right, and they don't know how, as silent dads have passed down the "Quiet Man" model to their sons.

Nonetheless, our emotions and the ability to communicate them remain the key to a healthy sex life. Effective communication between husband and wife provides knowledge on what is pleasing in the relationship, as well as understanding and security.

Christ wept openly with his friends over death and he expressed anger appropriately. Christ the carpenter and teacher was among the most manly of men. We must learn to model our lives after Jesus and to grow in our ability to open up about our feelings.

34

If we were able to walk around with Christ, we would see a man who was able to express a wide range of emotions. He was a natural at communicating on a feeling level. In John 2, we see a man with such strong anger he could throw out the money changers and yell, "How dare you turn My Father's house into a market!"

Imagine walking down a desert road on your way to a funeral of an old friend. Jesus sees His friend Mary and her friends weeping. He begins to feel Mary's pain; He begins to feel the pain of death. Christ knows He will raise Lazarus from the dead, yet He weeps. He weeps, He wails, He feels the deep pain of the human condition (John 11).

Picture yourself listening to Jesus as He tells you that the time for grieving is coming—that you will feel sad and depressed. He explains it in a way that makes grief seem normal. You realize that you can't run from the hurt. He says that this grieving will eventually turn to joy. Joy is the feeling of true happiness and contentment. That is what Jesus is describing in John 16. Sounds like a lot of emotional stuff going on.

Now you are in a garden; the sun is setting. Jesus has asked you and a couple of other men to join Him. He tells you His soul is overwhelmed with sorrow to the point of death

(Matthew 26:36–41). You sense the deep and intense emotions. Christ was and is able and unafraid to express those emotions.

HOLDING IN OUR FEELINGS

Men do have powerful feelings, and most of us would like to express our emotions. As noted earlier, though, our culture inhibits men from being themselves. There are many repercussions from this cultural inhibition. Men die younger than women and have more cardiac problems. Alcoholism, fetishes, pedophilia, voyeurism, and sexual addiction are all more prevalent among men than women. Less measurable but equally destructive is the inability to feel and to express emotions that has resulted from the cultural taboos on men regarding emotion. It is my belief that many of the sexual problems men struggle with are a direct result of their inability to feel and to deal with feelings constructively.

The healing power of feeling is clearly demonstrated in Carlos's life. At age six, Carlos found his father in bed with another woman. His father continually abused him both physically and verbally. Throughout his childhood, Carlos was in and out of mental institutions. In late adolescence, he had a homosexual experience that colored his behavior for years. He tried to prove himself with women and became a sexual addict. Then came the multiple relationships, multiple marriages, and multiple affairs as he searched for the perfect sex partner—someone who would make him feel complete.

Numerous affairs marked his last marriage. Yet, somehow in the emptiness of it, God reached Carlos, and he developed a personal relationship with Christ. He began to comprehend that his inability to feel was one of the root causes of his addiction. He not only struggled experiencing the emotions from his past, he didn't even understand how to communicate his present feelings. Without this ability to talk about his feelings, he would end up only creating more pain for himself.

Though now a Christian, Carlos still struggled with his sexual addiction. He understood the impact of his sin on his life and others. He sought Christian counsel and began to dig into the pain of his childhood—the anger at his father, his hurt for his mother. He felt the guilt and the shame. He screamed. He cried. He threw temper tantrums.

As the feelings came, he dealt with them. He was able to walk away from his affairs and begin communicating with his wife. The process of growing up had begun.

Like Carlos, all men need to express their feelings and communicate in order to experience a healthy sex life. Without communication, a sexual relationship will become meaningless and empty. The truth is that men desire to be open and honest and are willing to work hard at the struggle of communication.

DEALING WITH THE MYTH

Step 1: Understand that God is comfortable with our emotions. Pain, sorrow, sadness, and anger are not signs of spiritual immaturity. Ignore the pressures of church and society not to express so-called feelings of weakness. Christ is an example of how to handle and communicate our emotions. Remember that He expressed the full range of emotions while on earth, from grief and anger to joy. As a man, you also are free to do so.

Step 2: Practice communicating a wide range of feelings and situations to your girlfriend or wife. This will bring about a better understanding of who she is, and of course, she will understand you better. If you are single, this will allow you to know each other better and to evaluate the relationship and where you want it to go. If you are married, you can expect such expressions of your feelings to increase the joy of the sexual relationship.

Step 3: Meet with your wife weekly to discuss your feelings and struggles; generate a list of your feelings. Take this list of feelings and begin to work at understanding what is going on below the surface. Whether you are married or single, begin a journal to keep track of the feelings you experience.

As you consider your emotions, try to spot the root causes. For instance, if the emotion is anger, ask yourself what feeling might be causing the anger. Talk with other men about their feelings and how they express them.

Myth #5: Real Men Know How Women Think and Feel About Love and Romance

The myth goes something like this: Real men actually understand women emotionally, intellectually, and especially sexually. The reality, as most of us have experienced in relationships, is that men often find women confusing.

Consider Dan. He and his wife, Lynn, decided to seek counseling because of struggles due to the differences between men and women.

Such tensions are common for many couples.

Lynn seemed interested in sex during the first six months of marriage, but that interest faded as Dan and Lynn got busy with real life. Dan was beginning his career and sometimes seemed consumed by it. He was working hard for his lifestyle and his wife. He wanted to be a good provider.

Lynn was working but desired a family. Dan agreed to try to have children, although he would have liked to wait longer. Lynn believed children would bring her and Dan closer. She got pregnant and, in their second year of marriage, a baby was born.

Lynn's interest in sex and in Dan decreased even more that first year of parenthood, and this bothered him. He hoped she would read his mind and know his hurts and desires. Lynn was focused on her child and worn out from late-night feeding. She felt distant from Dan and interpreted his aloofness as avoidance. Her self-consciousness about being unattractive after the child furthered the gap, and Dan poured himself into his work.

Notice how the man and woman each interpreted the other's actions according to a certain set of motives. And each responded to the situation differently. This often has to do with different goals, perceptions, and motives that men and women have.

Soon a second child was on the way and Dan joked that each conception marked their only love-making. The relationship grew colder. Commitment and the hope of renewed closeness kept them together. The unaddressed struggles in the relationship and lack of communication resulted in a virtual absence of sexual intimacy. Lynn wanted to enjoy sex with Dan but she perceived Dan to be emotionally unavailable. Sex held no interest for her.

What caused their relationship to go cold? Though they thought they knew each other, they did not. Men and women are different in how they think, relate, and even talk.[10] Dan expected Lynn to know his desires without saying what those needs were. Lynn assumed Dan's physical distance meant he was avoiding her; Dan, though, felt he showed he loved her by working hard on the job to provide for her.

When Dan and Lynn came for marriage counseling, we focused on communicating their hurts. They discovered how they miscommunicated and misinterpreted, with all the pain those missteps bring. Forgiveness of the past and new ways to communicate began to heal their marriage.

As they talked on deeper levels, their sexual relationship began to grow. Lynn felt understood for the first time in the marriage. Dan found he could discuss his feelings and needs. He realized after sixteen years of marriage that Lynn did not think the same way he did. He thought she saw life the way he did and had the same sexual desires. Dan realized that Lynn was programmed differently. This knowledge was the beginning point for a healthier marriage.

Women, unlike men, connect through talking about feelings and being understood. We men sometimes struggle with listening and understanding. If there is a problem, we want to fix it. Guess what. Women usually don't share their struggles to get our advice. They want us to listen, understand, and share our own struggles with them. Weird, huh?

Not really. Women aren't weird, just different. And you can assure your wife that you're not weird either. You have different ways of responding; those ways are neither worse nor better than hers, just different. When men don't listen and try to understand, their wives can feel discounted or misunderstood. If that happens to your wife, she will usually lose her desire for sex altogether. Thankfully, the opposite is also true. Deep open communication can do wonders in solving sexual issues in a marriage.

We will never understand women fully. That's part of the excitement and mystery of our (and their) sexuality. Women differ from men in many ways. But if we can understand some basic facts about female sexuality, we can be more helpful and understanding to our wives. Here are six important truths—not myths—about female sexuality. Of course, these are generalizations from research, but my clinical experience and the testimonies of hundreds of women indicate that they are accurate.

1. Sex is less important to women. Not only do women need to be relationally and emotionally connected to be sexual, but they are less interested in sex. Women do not value sex as men do. They do not count the days between intercourse. Our wives do not see sex as a reflection on the state of the marriage.

2. Sex comes last. The level of talking, touching, and being close indicate the state of the marriage for the women. Sex tends to be way down the list of personal needs for the woman.

3. Women do not usually initiate sex. "Women send out signals that they are interested, but women are far less likely to actually say they want sex or make physical moves that say the same thing."[11] Men often complain that their wives do not initiate sex. A woman's concept of initiating sex might be to prepare a candlelight dinner and let the man take over from there. Being the initiator in the actual act of intercourse does not come naturally to most women.

4. *Women are not aroused by seeing male anatomy.* A swimsuit issue for women would not be a best-seller. In general, men are aroused by the feminine form; women are interested in a man's body after they know and care for his person.

5. *During sexual intimacy, women value the process and the follow-up.* Women are aroused by the touching and caressing of all parts of their bodies—not just genitals. They enjoy foreplay as much as sexual intercourse. A woman values the actual process of holding, being held and touched, and just being physically close.

She also likes being held closely after sex. During this time of "afterglow," she wants her man close to her, to talk softly or simply to lie at her side. A woman is turned off when her man rolls over and falls asleep after sex.

6. *Women are not concerned with performance.* Guess what, guys? Our wives are not consumed with how we

44

perform. For them it is the process, the connectedness they feel to us. Performance is secondary. If we get angry or apologize because we are not performing, problems can get bigger. Most women are not afraid to discuss performance and sexual problems with men.

Discussing these issues can be very threatening for men, who often find their masculinity threatened if they feel they were less than sexually potent. Yet, talking about them can be key to resolving many performance problems. And most women are willing to talk. But few will be concerned if their husbands' performance is diminished at times.

Understanding and communicating about these and other differences between your wife and you can lead to a healthy and mutually satisfying sexual life. Men and women can learn to love each other in ways that meet the needs of both.

Learning to do this can make us more complete. God made the two sexes to come together to form one in the bond of marriage. This oneness is meant to be relational, spiritual, emotional, and sexual.

DEALING WITH THE MYTH

Step 1: Admit your ignorance about your wife. Women are very different. Be willing to learn about the differences. It can be an enjoyable education.

Step 2: Do not expect your wife to respond to life the way you do. As noted earlier, she will not respond sexually the way a man responds sexually. Spend time discussing with your spouse how she views sex.

Step 3: Learn to enjoy the differences between the sexes. Do not make your main goal in the relationship to change the other person; rather, try to understand the differences. Remember, those differences are God-given. He has made men and women different to add zest to the relationship and a partner who can bring another perspective to life.

Step 4: Take this list about female sexuality and discuss it with your spouse. She may not agree with all six generalizations about women. Ask her which ones are true for her.

Step 5: Discuss with other men what they have learned about the differences between the sexes.

The Meaning of the Myths

You cannot ignore the implications of the five myths of male sexuality. Believing or acting on any one of the five has consequences for your relationship with your wife or girlfriend. In addition, accepting the first two myths can hurt your relationship to God, for those myths invite you to act in unfaithfulness to your wife.

Believing the five myths can lead us to danger in our relationships with our wives (or, if single, our girlfriends) and with our God.

Understanding these myths helps men realize that sex is not an adequate basis for relationship. We have been made in the image of God. Although that image has been damaged and distorted by sin, we can trust Christ to understand all struggles, even sexual temptation. Learning to communicate about sexual issues with our spouses and friends can be risky, but it's also very rewarding.

NOTES

1. Bernie Zilbergeld *The Truth About Man, Sex and Pleasure* (New York:Bantam, 1992), 43.

2. Michael Medved, *Hollywood vs. America* (Grand Rapids: Zondervan, 1992), 115.

3. Clifford Penner and Joyce Penner, *The Gift of Sex* (Waco, Tex.:Word, 1981), 26.

4. Tom W. Smith, "American Sexual Behaviors: Trends, Sociodemographic Differences, and Risk Behavior," a paper presented at the American Enterprise Institute, Washington, D.C., 18 October 1993. Smith was reporting results of the annual survey of the NORC, which measures social attitudes and behaviors to determine social trends in America.

5. Tom W. Smith as quoted in "Quotables," *Chicago Tribune*, 3 November 1993, A21. See also articles in *Chicago Sun-Times* 18 October 1993, 1; and *Chicago Tribune*, 19 October 1993, A4.

6. George Barna, *The Future of the American Family* (Chicago: Moody, 1993), 68.

7. "News Watch," *Washington Watch*, 29 October 1993, 2.

8. William Masters, Virginia Johnson, and Robert Kol, *Sex and Human Loving* (Boston: Little, Brown, 1986), 337.

9. Gary J. Oliver, *Real Men Have Feelings Too* (Chicago: Moody, 1993), 25.

10. Differences in communication styles between men and women often cause misunderstandings. See Deborah Tannen, *That's Not What I Meant* (New York: Ballantine, 1987).

11. Bernie Zilbergeld, *The Truth About Men, Sex and Pleasure* (New York: Bantam, 1992), 45.

Moody Press, a ministry of the Moody Bible Institute, is designed for education, evangelization, and edification. If we may assist you in knowing more about Christ and the Christian life, please write us without obligation: Moody Press, c/o MLM, Chicago, Illinois 60610.